STEP ONE

When Willpower Is Not Enough

Hazelden
Always, the pioneer

First published May, 1982

ISBN: 0-89486-151-4

Printed in the United States of America.

The following is an adaptation of one of the Twelve Steps in the program of Overeaters Anonymous. It is one person's interpretation and does not speak for the O.A. organization.

Are you a compulsive overeater?

What does it mean to be powerless over food and unable to manage your life? It might mean that you are 150 pounds overweight and in danger of losing your job as well as your health. It might mean that you spend a large percentage of your waking hours planning to diet, doing it for a while, going on a binge, once more outgrowing the clothes in your closet, and hating not only yourself but almost everyone around you. It might mean that you consume huge quantities of food, then vomit so that you won't gain weight, and live in constant fear that people will find out how crazy you are. It might simply mean that you spend so much time eating and/or thinking about food that the rest of your life is in a shambles.

If you are being controlled by an obsession with food, you probably know it at some level, even though you may not be ready to admit to yourself or anyone else. "Oh yes, I've put on a few pounds, but I can easily lose them if I set my mind to it — just a matter of finding the right diet and sticking to it."

We all tell ourselves this, when food and eating and weight are a problem, and we proceed to look for the perfect diet. Or we try to rearrange the circumstances around us so that we will be motivated to eat less. Some of the methods may work for a short time, but for the compulsive overeater none of them work very long.

How far do you have to go to hit bottom? Not far for some. Farther for others. The good news is that when we finally do admit that the problem is more than we can manage by ourselves, we have a place to go and a program that will lead us out of the mire of compulsive overeating.

The Twelve Steps of Overeaters Anonymous are the same as the Twelve Steps of Alcoholics Anonymous, substituting the word "food" for "alcohol." O.A. considers compulsive overeating to be an illness similar to alcoholism or drug addiction, and the Twelve Steps are a proven way to recovery.

Fat is a symptom of our illness. Although it is possible to overeat compulsively and not be fat, many of us come to O.A. because we don't like the way we look. We have tried to diet over and over, with little or no success. Our lives have become more and more chaotic and unhappy, and we feel that there must be a way out of the mess.

There is.

But in order to begin to get well, we need to admit that we are sick. It may be that you have been denying your problem with food for years. Do you eat alone when no one can see how much you consume? Do you hide secret stashes of goodies where only you can find them? Have you ever finished a complete dinner and then headed for the kitchen or the nearest food store to gulp down the equivalent of several more dinners?

To admit that we are powerless over food is difficult for most of us. What our instincts seem to demand is *more* power of every kind, not less. And food — the source of physical nourishment — seems such a good and necessary part of our existence. How can something so basic and so indispensible lead us astray?

There is nothing wrong with food, but there is something wrong with us when we cannot stop eating once we get started.

The first step to the recovery O.A. promises is to recognize that we are indeed incapable of managing our behavior when it comes to eating and food. Further, we admit that the disorder created by our compulsive overeating has spilled over into other areas of our lives, making them generally unmanageable. How can you manage your life if you don't know when you will be laid low by the next binge?

Gut-level acceptance

It is one thing to know intellectually that you have a problem with food. It is quite another to accept at a deep emotional level the fact that you are powerless to control what you eat. For most of us, gut-level acceptance of the fact that we are powerless over food comes only after repeated failure to prove that we can achieve control and be "normal."

Why can't we eat like other people? A snack here and there. A half piece of cake. A few potato chips. Moderation. Surely we can achieve it if we try hard enough. So we try again. And again. And each time we eventually fall flat on our faces into a binge.

Recovery begins when we admit defeat and declare bankruptcy. Until we do this, we are not ready to accept the kind of rigorous honesty that the O.A. program demands. As long as we deny that we have an illness over which we have no control — no more control than we would have over diabetes or measles — we will not be willing to maintain abstinence from compulsive overeating and work the Steps. Abstinence is not easy and neither are the Twelve Steps. Yet this is what has proved successful in arresting the illness and providing a basis for a new, satisfying, and productive life.

If you have tried enough other ways to stop overeating compulsively, you may be ready to agree with those of us who have found it to be true that there is no easier, softer way. On a gut level, this means submitting to a feeling of helplessness. "I quit; I throw in the sponge; I give up. I may have thought up until now that I could do almost anything I really put my mind to, but this has me licked. If it's up to my efforts alone, I can just resign myself to the fact that I will probably weigh 350 pounds and die an early death." The ego finally bows to the strength of forces beyond its control.

What about willpower?

Still not convinced that you are powerless over food? O.A. recommends that you go out and try a little controlled eating of a favorite food. Can you eat a little and stop? Can you have one dish of ice cream, put what remains of the carton back in the freezer, and leave it there? Or do you go back and finish what is left of the ice cream and then move on through the refrigerator, perhaps ending up with cold mashed potatoes?

Ah, but tomorrow will be different, right? Tomorrow you will get back on the diet and stick to it. No ice cream at all, just willpower. Some of us are able to stay on a diet for a period of time, but if we are compulsive overeaters we find that those periods of time get shorter and shorter as the illness progresses. The diet period dwindles to a week, a day, a morning, and then we may be bingeing around the clock.

Willpower is fine as far as it goes, but for the compulsive overeater it does not go far enough. The obsession we are trying to control is not rational, so it does not come under the sway of rational resolve. As a matter of fact, it is our "self-will run riot" that pushes us on from bite to bite all the way through a binge, so trying to use self-will to control compuslive overeating is like trying to put out a fire with gasoline. The driving force behind our white-knuckled, clenched-teeth "no" can just as well shift over and fuel the mania to swallow more and more and everything.

Much as we hate to admit it, an honest review of our behavior as compulsive overeaters shows clearly that in spite of the strongest resolve to stop overeating, we continue. Night after night we go to bed gorged and disgusted; we get up the next morning full of undigested food and fresh determination to maintain control; and usually before the day is over, we have done it again — no amount of willpower is able to pull us out of the quicksand.

How about changing the circumstances?

"If my mother had not over-fed me when I was a baby, I would not be programmed to overeat." "If I had someone who loved me enough, I wouldn't need all this extra food." "If I didn't have so many problems and wasn't so tense and upset all the time, I could eat less." "Maybe if I move to another city, I can lose weight." "If I get another job, or a wife, or a divorce, or more money . . . if only . . . maybe . . . if . . ."

It is tempting to think that we can cure compulsive overeating by changing our environment and altering the circumstances we don't like. We think we could stop eating too much if we could somehow make ourselves happy. Unhappiness causes us to overeat, so we may believe. Actually, it is the other way around. Overeating makes us unhappy, whatever the external circumstances.

Did you think that you would stop overeating when you graduated from high school and got away from that pressure? When you finally found a good job? When you got married? And were you surprised when the same old pattern repeated itself in the new situation? You may not have been all that surprised, but you probably sank deeper into despair.

Blaming our misery on the people and situations around us, we frantically try to manipulate them in order to produce the perfect environment. In the process, we often make things worse instead of better. And we are still overeating. Suppose you decide it's your boring job that makes you think about food and eating all the time. You find a job that appears to be more interesting. But instead of being able to concentrate on the new job, you are so controlled by the progressive compulsion that you cannot give full attention to the work, and you live in constant fear of being fired. Or maybe you can cope with the demands of the job, but you binge every night when you get home. So you decide it's your apartment that needs to be changed, or your husband.

Even if it were possible to pinpoint an exact reason for eating compulsively, it might very well be that the circumstance is something which is impossible to change. Then what do you do? Through the O.A. program, we learn that we often cannot change external conditions but we can be changed inside ourselves.

Powerless over persons, places and things

Along with admitting that we are powerless over food, most of us have come to the conclusion that we are also powerless over persons, places, and things. We have tried to manipulate them to suit our whims but have not succeeded. Trying to control life has made us uptight, fearful, frustrated, and often furious. What a relief to admit that we cannot manage even our own lives! Then we are able to drop the exhausting burden of trying to make everything go the way we want it to go. Attempting to do that is like trying to push water uphill. It is a great relief to give up the attempt.

When we take Step One, we stop wearing ourselves out with futile efforts. We admit that we are in the grips of forces beyond our control — first of all an obsession with food and secondly the vicissitudes of life. Events will take their course, the people around us will demand their rights to behave as individuals, and what others do may very well be exactly the opposite of what we would advise.

Letting go is what frees us in the long run, but it is frequently a very hard thing to do. Some of us need to be beaten down pretty far before we are willing to relax our useless mental and emotional efforts to control external circumstances. Step One is often not taken until the compulsive overeater has been devastated and defeated over and over again, not only by food but by life itself.

Powerless every day

Most of us find that we do not take Step One once and for all. It is something we do repeatedly, often on a daily basis. Since denial and self-deception are a part of the illness, we can easily forget that we are compulsive overeaters. This is extremely dangerous.

We don't like the idea of being different from other people. Why shouldn't we be able to eat everything? Well-meaning family and friends can contribute to the self-deception. "It won't hurt you to have one little piece of birthday cake." "You're not overweight. How can you be a compulsive overeater?" "You've been doing so well, you deserve a reward." "Life is too short to deny yourself pleasure."

Life will be even shorter if we kill ourselves with food, and there is little pleasure in the after-effects of a binge. A compulsive overeater *is* different in that he or she is always one bite away from a binge. This is what we need to remember every day.

How we got this way is irrelevant. We are not "bad" people. We are addicted to overeating, especially certain foods, in the same way as an alcoholic is addicted to alcohol. We cannot eat spontaneously, on impulse, because once we get started we don't know when we will be able to stop. There is no need to judge ourselves or feel guilty — this is a disease, just as alcoholism and diabetes are diseases.

Similarly, there is no cure for compulsive overeating. It is our experience that no real compulsive overeater ever becomes a normal eater. Once the line is crossed, there is no return. Those of us who have tried going back to "normal eating" have sooner or later found out through harsh and devastating experience that we are still one bite away from a binge. Without the control that comes through the O.A. program, we are lost.

Paradoxically, the control we gain through the program is given to us when we stop *trying* to manage the food obsession and our lives, and let go of both. Through our weakness comes strength. As long as we think we can do it ourselves by willpower, it is our experience that we continue to fail. Every day.

How many days have you gotten up in the morning full of determination to make this a perfect diet day? How many times have you succeeded? If you are like most of us, without outside help the successful diet days become fewer and fewer and the binges get worse.

So why do we fight taking the First Step and admitting that the situation is beyond our control? Most of us are brought up to think that we should be able to handle our problems and manage our lives independently. Not to be able to do this is to be weak. To say we are powerless over anything goes against all of our conditioning. Besides, giving up control requires giving up the idea of doing things our way. "My way" as a compulsive overeater usually means discovering some secret formula that will enable me to eat what I want, as much as I want, and still lose weight.

Every day, we compulsive overeaters need to remember that our old ways did not work, that we are powerless over food and our appetites and the habit of overeating.

Isn't there another way?

Is there something besides abstinence and the Twelve Steps which you think might work for you? An exercise club? Hypnosis? Eating one meal a day? Fasting? A new diet? If you still think there has to be an easier, softer way, then you probably are not ready to take the Steps or willing to live without your favorite binge foods.

Most of us come to Overeaters Anonymous as a last resort when all else has failed. For someone who uses food as a tranquilizer to dull the pain of living, the idea of abstinence is frightening. A specified number of planned meals (usually three) per day with nothing in between and no binge foods may seem impossible. Probably none of us would be willing to consider abstinence if it were not for the fact that everything else we tried sooner or later failed to solve our eating problem. When we have exhausted all other methods of controlling compulsive overeating, we become desperate enough to concede defeat.

Some of us are able to identify with the stories we hear from other compulsive overeaters whose disease has progressed farther than our own. A sudden flash of insight may show us where we are headed if our own illness is not arrested. We may recognize similarities in our own behavior to what is described as an early stage in someone else's disease. "There but for the grace of God go I." You may be only ten pounds overweight, or not overweight at all, and still be powerless to control the compulsion to overeat. Sneak eating, a preoccupation with food, periodic binges followed by remorse — these are the signs of a developing problem which if untreated inevitably gets worse, not better.

Slow destruction

"Okay," you say. "I do eat too much. I have a closet full of clothes in just about every size, and almost everything is too small. But I'm not hurting anyone except myself. If I want to eat my way into an early grave, that's my business. There are many worse things I could be doing." True enough. There are faster ways of killing yourself.

And what about the effects of your overeating on the people around you? What kind of a mood are you in when you have been bingeing for several hours and a child asks for help with homework? What do you say to your boyfriend when he asks you to an impromptu dinner and you have just eaten a large box of cookies? How many times have you picked a fight with your spouse because you were disgusted with yourself? Does she or he want a divorce because all you do at night is eat and watch television?

Are you living your life the way you want to live it? Or is the compulsion to overeat gradually destroying you emotionally and spiritually, as well as physically? How much energy and enthusiasm do you have? For a compulsive overeater who continues to overeat, the answer to this last question is usually less and less.

Drunk on food

Do you "need" extra food the way an alcoholic "needs" a drink? Between meals or right after eating a complete dinner, do you crave something more? Is the craving uncontrollable? Does the desire for more drive you to keep on eating long after your body's legitimate need for nourishment has been taken care of?

Though it may sound strange, it is possible to be drunk on too much food. Compulsive overeaters attest to passing out during a binge, especially when eating large quantities of refined sugar. Getting drunk on food produces a high, followed by a stupor, followed by a hangover. After a binge, sleep is apt to be disturbed. Indigestion, sweating, and a racing mind are common phenomena. You wake up the next morning feeling as though you've been hit over the head, barely able to get out of bed and drag through the day.

While bingeing, you are out of touch with reality and the rest of the world. After bingeing, you do not have much to give to other people, to your work, or even to some sort of activity that might normally be fun. Overeating saps energy, to say nothing of ruining your disposition. You do and say crazy things that you don't really mean. A compulsive overeater can get drunk on food night after night, day after day.

Like the alcoholic, the overeater gets caught up in a futile quest for satisfaction. Consuming more and more, he or she never achieves that magic satiety. No matter how much food is eaten, satisfaction continues to elude the seeker. It is always in the next bite.

A life-giving program

To anyone who has experienced the chaos and confusion which goes along with compulsive overeating, the ability to have three meals a day — period — is a miraculous change. Binges take time and energy. There is the time and attention spent thinking about what and when and how much one will or will not eat. There is the time spent procuring the food and consuming it. And then there is the time spent recovering from the binge. As this activity increases, it crowds out other interests and concerns. Life can eventually become a constant round of eating and remorse, with hardly any time or energy left for anything else.

Taking Step One is the beginning of a new life. Followed honestly, the O.A. program promises faith and enthusiasm in place of despair — a transformation which is happening to people every day. You can go to meetings all over the country and find examples of changed lives — inside as well as outside. The program works if we work it. Step by Step we grow when we are willing to first acknowledge our need for help and then be open to new ways of thinking and acting. There are no failures with the program, only slow successes.

Admitting that we are powerless makes us ready to change. Our attitude changes from one of defiance and denial to one of surrender. "Yes, I am a compulsive overeater. I am powerless over food and my life has become unmanageable." We stop fighting the disease and the fact that we have it. This attitude of surrender is a prerequisite to recovery. According to the "Big Book"* of Alcoholics Anonymous, pride and self-centered fear are our worst enemies. The ego must surrender if we are to get well.

Surrender will grow and bear fruit as we continue through the Twelve Steps. By means of abstinence, we stop using excess food as a way of trying to solve or avoid the problems of life. Slowly but surely, confusion is replaced by order and inner peace. Where before we were full of fear, we become confident and productive. Out of weakness and the admission of utter defeat comes strength.

---

* *Alcoholics Anonymous,* published by A.A. World Services, New York, NY. Available through Hazelden Educational Materials.

Honesty

A program that requires rigorous honesty sounds forbidding. Probably no one would be willing to undertake abstinence and the Twelve Steps except as a last resort — as the only way to be free of the obsession with food and eating.

Honesty *is* the foundation of recovery. We begin to get honest with ourselves when we admit that we have a problem with food. How many of us blame obesity on a faulty metabolism or glands? "I don't know why I can't lose weight. I hardly eat anything." Anything that anybody *sees* us eat, that is.

If you are a closet-eater, you have lots of company. Bingeing in private is part of the disease. If no one sees us eat it, it doesn't count — right? We cheat on our diets and we may be cheating in other areas of life, too. Certainly, we are cheating ourselves out of health and happiness, to say nothing of self-respect and peace of mind.

First we get honest about the fact that we are compulsive overeaters. Some of us can remember sneak-eating as children and denying what we had done when confronted with the evidence. We may have blamed the disappearance of the food on someone else, perhaps the dog if no other person was around.

We don't like to admit weakness even, and especially, to ourselves. It's hard to face the truth. Running away from it can be a conditioned response. How often do you try to escape painful reality, or what appears to be boring reality, by having something to eat? Some of us have used alcohol and drugs along with excess food to try to dull the inevitable pain of living.

In the long run, being dishonest and trying to escape hurts more than facing the truth. The more we avoid reality, the more fearful we become. Pushing down a hurt with a mountain of food does not cure the hurt or make it go away. Whatever we use to drug ourselves, we end up with an additional problem — the harmful effects of abuse.

Large quantities of unnecessary calories can produce a sedating effect for awhile, both physically and emotionally. But an honest appraisal will reveal the harm that is being done to body, emotions, and spirit. It's hard to think straight during or after a binge.

The beauty of the Twelve Step program is that it provides a support system to help us get honest. We learn honesty from each other. It's a lot easier to face and admit compulsive overeating in a group of people who are doing the same thing and who are sharing their experience, strength, and hope. Before coming to the program, many of us felt that we were the only people in the world who did such crazy things with food, and our isolation produced more suffering.

Beyond Step One, honesty is the basis of the other eleven Steps. We can't work this program and delude ourselves for very long. Now don't panic. The truth about ourselves comes to us in gradual stages, as we become ready to accept it. We don't have to face it all at once, nor could we. We each have an individual inner pattern of growth which unfolds as we go along.

Sometimes it hurts to face the truth instead of escaping into food. Sometimes we have to hurt in order to get well. In the long run, it is the truth that frees us from compulsion.

The turning point

Rather than face our powerlessness over persons, places, situations, and life in general, we reached for a prop, something we thought would give us power or something that made us feel powerful temporarily — or at least less powerless. Then we became dependent on the prop. We can be dependent on alcohol, other drugs, harmful relationships — a variety of crutches which eventually hinder our progress rather than help us. Some of us become dependent on excess food.

The turning point in the life of a compulsive overeater comes with the realization that one has a fatal disease and that without help he or she will be controlled by its progression. The "need" for more and more food to dull emotional pain and escape problems has put us in the position of an addict. Once we recognize the priority of the illness, we are ready to give wholehearted attention to the means of arresting it.

When we are convinced emotionally as well as intellectually that our lives depend on recovering from compulsive overeating, we become willing to go to any lengths to get well. The O.A. program throws out a lifeline. Grabbing it and hanging on means going to meetings, getting a sponsor, calling in a food plan, learning to maintain abstinence, working the Steps, and staying in contact with the group. Sometimes schedules need to be rearranged and other activities changed. Sometimes relationships are reevaluated. We learn how to avoid situations that get us into trouble. We become willing to do whatever needs to be done in order to stay abstinent and work the program. Where life before may have been very complicated, the new one is often much more simple! Giving priority to the requirements of recovery helps to sort out everything else.

No longer will our lives be controlled by the desire for more and more food. We are going to learn how to function productively and happily without hiding in the refrigerator. The Twelve Steps guide us in getting rid of harmful dependencies and developing according to an inner pattern of positive growth. Too good to be true? We may think so until we have been in the program long enough to see with our own eyes the evidence of changed lives. We will hear stories of how despair and anxiety gradually turned to faith and confidence. We will see people living in new bodies with new mental and emotional outlooks to match.

One step at a time; one day at a time. We become new people not by willpower or by altering our environment but by first admitting that our ways have not worked and that we need help. Empty hands are necessary in order to receive the gifts of the program.